WILD
WEASELS

WILD WEASELS

ELITE RADAR – KILLERS OF THE USAF

TONY THORNBOROUGH
FRANK B MORMILLO

OSPREY
AEROSPACE

Published in 1992 by
Osprey Publishing Limited
59 Grosvenor Street London W1X9DA

ISBN 1 85532 206 4

Editor Dennis Baldry
Page design Paul Kime
Printed in Hong Kong

Front cover Riding on a rocket
plume, an F-4G Phantom II lets loose
a 'Scene Mag' Hughes AGM-65B
Maverick precision-guided missile.
The weapon packs a modest 125 lb
high-explosive warhead, but its
kinetic energy is devastating.
Infrared-guided D-models also form
part of the Weasel's extensive
armoury (*USAF*)

Back cover Home from the range. A
35th TFW F-4G Weasel is directed
into its parking slot at George AFB,
California, after completing a mock
'battle of the beams' over the
electronic warfare range at Tonopah,
Nevada (*Frank B Mormillo*)

Title page A selection of Wild
Weasel patches

Right On 21 November 1966 the
first four of half a dozen North
American F-100F Super Sabres
specially adapted to the new Wild
Weasel I radar-hunting mission were
deployed from Eglin AFB, Florida, to
steamy Korat RTAFB, Thailand — the
stop-gap vanguard pending the
introduction of the much faster
Republic EF-105F Thunderchief in the
Weasel role. Despite losing two
aircraft to hostile fire and an
additional aircraft to 'operational
causes', the F-100 'Huns' proved the
Wild Weasel concept: US aircraft
losses fell immediately by a factor of
seven. Its crews returned to Nellis,
Nevada, to establish the 'Willie
Weasel College', and its graduates
would later go to war in the EF-105F
and the F-105 'Thud'. This Hun saw
out its last days with the Texas Air
National Guard (*Theodore Van Geffen*)

For a catalogue of all books published by Osprey Aerospace
please write to:

**The Marketing Department,
Octopus Illustrated Books, 1st Floor, Michelin House,
81 Fulham Road, London SW3 6RB**

Introduction

The Wild Weasels were created during the height of the air war in Southeast Asia to meet the stringent and hazardous job of suppressing the new generation of Soviet-designed, radar-directed anti-aircraft systems. To fulfil the task, off-the-shelf jets were kitted with sophisticated superheterodyne and interferometric receivers which 'sniffed' the airwaves in search of hostile radars, enabling the skilled crew of two – composed of an intrepid stick and his signal-deciphering EWO or Bear buried in the 'pit' behind – to acquire and lock-up on the target dish, and then go in for the kill with CBUs and ARMs.

Adopting the tradename 'First In, Last Out', the profession reached its zenith in the post-Vietnam years with the introduction of the purpose-converted McAir F-4G Advanced Wild Weasel V, arguably the ultimate expression of the Phamous Phantom. This subsequently became the most numerous of the metal *mustelids* and provided the leading edge of the suppression of enemy air defences (SEAD) forces during Operation Desert Storm, where the three squadrons distributed between Shaika Isa in Bahrain and Incirlik, Turkey, flew around the clock and lobbed over 1500 radar-zapping missiles to the Bears' war cry 'Magnum!', achieving devastating results.

So successful were they that plans to retire the force as an economy move have now been suspended, and three dozen of the venerable F-4G will continue to soldier on with the Air National Guard until suitable replacements can be integrated into the new superwings: the F-16C 'Electric Jet' equipped with the HTS pod (known as 'Weasel in a Can'!), and the more capable, specially adapted twin-seat F-15E/G/Eagle. Hostile radars and communications arrays will remain the priority targets in any future conflict, so their operators would be well-advised to take heed of the warning: 'Cave Putorium'! The Weasels will be there to take them out.

Many old hands in the community and their peers elsewhere in the USAF, along with numerous other people, lent a guiding hand in the compilation of this book over the course of the past few years and the authors and publishers wish to express their sincere thanks to them all, and especially: MSgt Rolf Carter, Peter E Davies, Lt Michele DeWerth, SSgt Michael Dugre, Christian Gerard, John J Harty, Col Thomas A Hornung, Ben Knowles, SSgt Robert E Lee, Lindsay T Peacock, Maj Emerson W Pittman, SSgt William M Rhodes, Maj Brian C Rogers, Maj James E Rotramel, Maj 'Jerry' Stiles (Ret), Capt Mike Turner, Capt James Tynan and Lt Col Jim Uken.

Tony Thornborough and Frank B Mormillo, Bristol, England, and Covina, California, September 1991

Right Enjoying a respite between combat operations at Takhli RTAFB, Thailand, in May 1970 while assigned to the 354th TFS 'Bulldogs' and bearing the appropriate nickname *SAM fighter*, EF-105F Thunderchief 63-8311 represents one of the second wave of Weasels deployed to the war zone in Southeast Asia. The Thuds numerous SAM-site kills testify to its potency (*Barry Miller via Jim Rotramel*)

Contents

Cave Putorium

Right Reinforcements in the form of the 12th TFS Weasels arrived at Korat RTAFB, Thailand from Kadena, Okinawa on 24 September 1970. The unit was consolidated with the 355th TFW Weasel Thuds and redesignated the 6010th WWS. The JB codes were adopted when the aircraft became part of the 17th WWS, 388th TFW, in December of the following year. The assymetric load of Standard ARM (Anti-Radiation Missile), Shrike, electronic countermeasures (ECM) and external fuel tanks was typical of the era (*Don Logan via Jim Rotramel*)

Above Wearing its war-weary camouflage, a svelte Weasel Thud and its crew amble along the ramp at Korat, Thailand. Thunderchiefs became all-up F-105G radar-destroyers after the application of no fewer than five related Technical Orders (known simply as TO's). During its earlier years with the 357th TFS, 63-8301 was decorated with the names *Moonlighter* and *Jinkin' Josie* (*Don Logan via Jim Rotramel*)

Above *Draggin' Ass* behind a tanker. Operations shifted from Loas back towards North Vietnam during the harrowing summer and fall of 1972 as President Nixon unleashed the full fury of US airpower against Hanoi, and this Shrike-toting machine assigned to Detachment 1 of the 561st TFS was one of the vanguard, redeployed from McConnell AFB, Kansas, on 7 April as part of *Constant Guard I*. Combat ops commenced five days later (*Hoynacki via Jim Rotramel*)

Right Sabre-toothed Thud brandishes its teeth in November 1972. The multitude of protrusions are associated with the KA-71 combat camera and direction-finding Radar Homing & Warning Systems (*Barry Miller via Jim Rotramel*)

Left Sittin' pretty after some serious SAM-Busting, 62-4434 nestles in among other Det 1 561st TFS and some 17th WWS Thuds at Korat ... (*via Jim Rotramel*)

Above ... and the same machine assigned to the 17th 'Wild Weasel' Squadron, a year later. Nicknamed *Snaggle Tooth*, it bears the unusual ADU-315 dual-Shrike arrangement fitted for extra radar-busting power. Today, twenty years on, this aircraft is a non-flying resident at RAF Lakenheath in Suffolk, England. After having suffered the ignominy of acting as Battle Damage Repair Article, it was partially restored and resprayed on the orders of the Base Commander, an ex-Thunderchief pilot! (*via Jim Rotramel*)

Overleaf Thunderchiefs on the wing. The F-105G at rear was appropriately nicknamed *Northbound* and was assigned to Maj 'Lucky' Eckman, who completed 200 combat sorties over North Vietnam. In all, forty-six Wild Weasel Thuds were shot down during the Vietnam war, but the radar sites they destroyed amounted to three figures. Many expatriate North Vietnamese SAM operators who fled their country still jolt with fear at the word 'Weasel'! (*Barry Miller via Jim Rotramel*)

Above The 66th Weasel Weapons Squadron – the 'Willie Weasel School' – evolved from the 4537th Combat Crew Training Squadron, formed at Nellis in 1966. The Aerospace Ground Equipment supporting these pristine Thuds nine years later are as spick-and-span as the aircraft (*Frank B Mormillo*)

Left Mounting the F-105G Wild Weasel III involved a long climb to the spacious cockpit. The Bears rated the 'Thud Weasel's' cockpit ergonomics as one of the best-organized in the family before the arrival of the F-4G Phantom (*Frank B Mormillo*)

Above With exhaust airbrakes in the 'at ease' position, a checkertailed 66th WWS Thud soaks up the sun at Nellis. Most of the unit's Thunderchiefs were eventually reassigned to the new 'Home of the Wild Weasels', as George's placard proudly proclaimed. The switchover started in 1973 and took two years to complete, as machines and crews returned home from SE-Asia (*Frank B Mormillo*)

Above right The F-105 possessed stalky, but solid landing gear. Its razorlike intakes were one of Republic's more adventurous innovations. When this photo was taken, several of the aircraft had clocked-up 6000 hours (*Frank B Mormillo*)

Below right 'Zoom!' A Nellis-based Thud tucks up its gear outbound for the ranges, red beacons flashing to announce its departure (*Don Logan via Ben Knowles*)

Golf at George

George, the Californian 'High Desert Base' located near Victorville, had assumed the role of 'Weasel College' for both the Thud and snub-nosed Phantom by 1975. Changing a Thud's Pratt & Whitney J75-P-19W turbojet meant unbolting the entire rear fuselage. Attached and detached tails form the subject of this artistic perspective of the apron at George AFB in November 1975 (*Ben Knowles*)

Above George's famous *Hanoi Hustler* on the ramp in June 1978. After retirement, the aircraft was placed on exhibit at the Air Force Museum in Dayton, Ohio. It was flown in by Maj Jim Boyd and Capt Gary Crystal. (*Frank B Mormillo*)

Left The Weasel Thud's ear-splitting J75 turbojet produced 26,400 lb st with water injection, which generated an extra ton of thrust on takeoff. The aircraft was noted for its 'hard light'. The mighty tail stood a fraction over 20 ft above the ground (*Frank B Mormillo*)

Above The Thud destroyed 29 MiGs during the Vietnam War, and F-105G 63-8320, nicknamed *Hanoi Hustler*, allegedly claimed three of them, including one that was reportedly knocked out of the sky when it ran into the bomb rack that *Cooter* (one of nicknames assigned to '320 when serving with the 333rd 'Lancers' during the conflict) jettisoned while under pursuit! (*Frank B Mormillo*)

Left Cart-starts are a messy but effective way of getting the turbines in motion. Compressed air, piped through a chunky hose from a starter trolley, was more often used (*Brian C Rogers*)

By 1975 the 35th TFW was flying two operational squadrons of F-105Gs: the 561st, under the command of Lt Col Don Yates, and the 562nd, initially headed by Lt Col David Perry. Both men, in common with the bulk of their squadron peers, were veterans of the arduous war in SE Asia (*Bill Mallerba via Jim Rotramel*)

The F-105G in its element: fast, sleek and powerful! The blue STARM is an inert example used for practice 'lock-ups' on 'enemy' radar sites. The live version could be fired in a turn and could be in-flight tuned to home down the throat of a radar operating at any frequency range within the limits of its broad-band Maxson seeker head. 62-4442 carried the artwork *Muttley the Flying Dog – Tee Hee Hee* during the latter stages of the Vietnam war, a spin-off from Hanna Barbera's 'Dick Dastardly' cartoon series (*via Jim Rotramel*)

Above An F-105G from the 561st TFS retracts its legs after executing a missed approach over George in June 1978. The 'coke-bottle' (area-ruled) Thud itself could manage 1386 mph and a ceiling of 52,000 ft when 'clean'. Down in the weeds with the burner engaged, Republic's masterpiece could slice through the sound barrier with ease – it may have given the Vietnamese rice paddies a nasty jolt, but kept the nimble MiGs off their tail (*Frank B Mormillo*)

Above right Thud! Republic's F-105 'Ultra Hog' was not one to float along the runway in ground effect, hence the unflattering onomatopoeic sobriquet. Takeoff, by contrast, was ponderous and crews joked that if Republic Aviation were able, they would design an aircraft that would require a runway which circled the Earth! (*Frank B Mormillo*)

Below right Republic built 143 twin-seat F-105F Thunderchiefs, of which some 60 were brought up to full F-105G 'Wild Weasel III' standard. At the close of hostilities in SE Asia, a mere 61 twin-seaters remained in service, including 44 Weasels and 17 of the 'vanilla' F model. The most notable distinguishing feature of the 'Golf' was the Quick Reaction Capability-380 blisters bolted to its flank, which housed AN/ALQ-105 and AN/ALT-28 electronic countermeasures (*Frank B Mormillo*)

Linebackers

Right One of the premier F-4C Weasel outfits was the 67th TFS 'Supercocks' based at Kadena AB, Okinawa. The unit was TDY'ed to Korat in time for the Linebacker II offensive against North Vietnam in December 1972, and their chief tactic was to lob Shrike missiles in a standoff mode (*Katsuhiko Tokunaga via Ben Knowles*)

Below) One of the best-known F-4C Weasels durin the war years was 63-7470, which carried the nickname *Rub a dub-dub, three men in a tub*. The acronym on the nosegear door stands for 'You Gotta be sh + + + + me'(!) and was carried by most of the squadron's aircraft. Other nicknames of note included *Brain Damage, Super Cocks Swiss SAMlar* and *Jail Bait,* which reflected the rigour and danger of the Weasel mission in combat. The large yellow access gantry was used for maintenance (*Harley Copic via Jim Rotramel*)

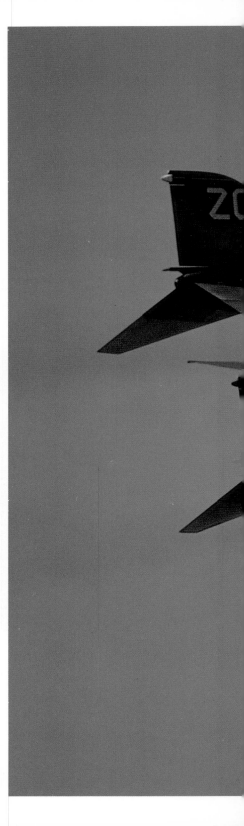

Above The Stateside Replacement Training Unit was located initially at Nellis alongside the Weasel Thunderchief college. This nostalgic shot depicts '815 with arrestor hook anchoring the beast to a dusty desert (*Ben Knowles*)

Left After completing some 460 combat sporties, the 67th TFS returned to Kadena. *Rub a dub-dub* adopted the 18th TFW's 'Zulu-Zulu' tailcode and special markings are confined to the Firebee drone kill – somewhat different prey from North Vietnamese radar sites! (*via Ben Knowles*)

Above A tidy flightline of Wild Weasel IVs at George. The cockpit configurations, however, varied considerably between the aircraft. The F-4C Weasel came about rather hectically during the war period and suffered many changes before it finally worked. Individual aircraft boasted a pick-'n'-mix kit of 'sniffers', taken from the gamut of devices which included the basic Phantom AN/APR-25 & -26 RHAWS and launch-warning receivers, the ER-142, Bendix AN/APS-107, along with Applied Technology's digitally-enhanced derivatives (*Frank B Mormillo*)

Above right *Old Smoky* in action, bound for the SADS (simulated air defence sites) at Nellis's Caliente Range. George's 35th TFW became 'Home of the Wild Weasels' during 1975 and provided Weasel RTU facilities for both Thud and Phantom pilots and Bears; graduates from the F-105G 'programme' were subsequently assigned to the 561st or 562nd Tactical Fighter Squadrons, and those from the F–4C 'programme' to the 67th TFS at Kadena, or 81st TFS at Spangdahlem (*Frank B Mormillo*)

Below right Thirty-six F-4Cs drawn from McAir production Blocks 16-24 were adapted to the defence-suppression mission between 1966 and 1970. The definitive 'kit' included AN/ALR-46 and -53 radar receivers which provided threat type and azimuth only – a far cry from the follow-on F-4G. Weaponry revolved around Shrikes and cluster bombs. Crews headed towards the target radar dish and trusted that the Shrike would 'lock-up' *before* they found themselves sitting on top of a SAM complex! (*Frank B Mormillo*)

Above USAFE's dedicated Wild Weasel IVs comprised the 81st TFS 'Panthers' who operated a dozen F-4Cs out of Spangdahlem AB, Germany, and who came into being at the base on 15 January 1973. The hotch-potch collection of F-4Cs were withdrawn from active use during 1978–79 when many were handed over to the Indiana Air National Guard at Terra Haute and Fort Wayne – though neither of the latter flew the aircraft in the Weasel mission. These machines were the only F-4C Phantoms to possess an ECM pod capability, as evidenced by this beast which totes a Westinghouse AN/ALQ-119 deception jammer (*Alec J Molton via Ben Knowles*)

Left The insignia of the 35th TFW dominates this wide-angle perspective. Backseat Bears clambered in and out of the aircraft by means of the intake duct, vari-ramp and pilot's steps. George's F-4C Weasel RTU was the 39th TFTS 'Cobras', reactivated at the base on 1 July 1977 (*Frank B Mormillo*)

Farewell Ol' Friends

Left A pair of becalmed 562nd TFS Thunderchiefs soaking up the sun at George AFB. The rugged Thud had a max takeoff weight of 54,580 lb, which used up about a mile and a half of runway! The ground-pounding sound is one of yesteryear (*Frank B Mormillo*)

Below Just for show: captive, inert, practice munitions comprising 'slicks', STARM and Shrike strapped to a 562nd TFS Thunderchief at George in October 1979. Thuds started to carry the new codes that summer (*Frank B Mormillo*)

'Okay guys, bare your teeth — now!' Few can forget the thunder and glamour of Republic's 'Ultra Hog'. Not to be outdone by the new Weasels in town, during their twilight months George's F-105Gs began to sprout huge sharkmouths. Much-loved by those who flew her, the Thud epitomized American aero engineering of the late fifties and soldiered on in the frontline until July 1980 (*Brian C Rogers*)

Above July 1980 and a 562nd TFS Thunderchief taxies-in following one of the last F-105G sorties to be flown by the 35th TFW. Another tail, number 62-4416, was kept at George AFB as a memorial to former Thud pilots (*Frank B Mormillo*)

Right Thunderchief: symbol of freedom to a whole generation of American fighter pilots (*Frank B Mormillo*)

Slatted Rhinos

Right The original Wild Weasel V set against the picturesque backdrop of the rugged terrain at Ogden Logistics Center, Hill AFB, Utah. F-4E 69-7254 served as initial testbed for the AN/APR-38A Homing & Warning computer and its myriad antennae, beginning in December 1975. Conversion was tackled under two phases: Group A, or Time Compliance TO 1F-4E-600, involved the structure and wiring; while 1F-4G-501 provided for installation of the Group B HAWC. According to the programme manager John Harty there were over 100 special retrofit drawings and 250 + pages of data to describe the mods (*Brian C Rogers*)

Below The 35th TFW received its first F-4G on 28th April 1978 when Colonel Dudley J Foster, Wing CO, and his 'pitter' Capt Dennis B Haney, brought tail 69-0239 into gentle contact with George's runway. Deliveries proceeded at a steady rate of three per month. 69-0240, the main subject here and the eighth in the series, was delivered on 3 June that year (*Frank B Mormillo*)

Tail number 69-7208 was dedicated to the City of Victorville, up the road from George AFB. It was also the sixteenth Block 42-45 F-4E to be converted to the task by the Logistics Command at Ogden OOALC, hence the romantic *Sweet Sixteen*. The initial batch of 116 F-4Gs were rebuilt using 118 conversion kits: Nos 1 and 27 were both applied to '254 (latterly during the early months of 1979, when it went in for deep maintenance and was brought up to the 'production' standard), while No 89 was not installed in any aircraft. McAir reworked the first two examples, 69-7254 & -7263; the rest were handled by the OOALC. Each F-4E-to-G 'sex change' took an average of 14,420 manhours spread out over a 'through flow' of some 110 days, and cost an average of $2.8 million – the price of an original F-4E in FY 1969 dollars! (*Frank B Mormillo*)

Right 'Red Squadron' was the 563rd 'Aces', and one of its birds is all angles and dangles – the typical parked posture. The all-moving tail serves primarily to provide pitch control; roll authority is furnished by pop-up spoilers on the wing (*Frank B Mormillo*)

Above Not a failed engine, but the crew chiefs at work at the dispersal. Phased Maintenance Inspections and other work required 'pulling' the aircraft out of the apron at 150 hour intervals for treatment in the hangars. 'Organizational' maintenance involved 'hands-on' work on the flightlines, and each crew chief was assigned his or her own personal charge. Aircraft underwent deep maintenance at Ogden OOALC every 54 months, the same frequency as that required for the F-4E and RF-4C (*Frank B Mormillo*)

Above General Dynamics Pomona built the long-range Standard ARM missile, capable of picking-off radars at a range of up to 35 miles. The STARM made its combat debut in March 1968 and in its definitive AGM-78D format was the primary standoff weapon of the F-4G in the early days, interfaced with the Weasel's sensitive receivers. Block 60 + Israeli F-4Es also possess a STARM capability (*Frank B Mormillo*)

Right A pair of 'Aces' scream across George in March 1980. By that time the tailcodes were painted in sombre black (*Frank B Mormillo*)

Dobbins' Thuds

Right All teeth, the 116th TFW ready themselves for takeoff. Guardsmen form a third of all TAC's muscle, but the Georgia ANG located near Atlanta has to date been the only part-time outfit to fly the Wild Weasel mission, such is its specialised nature. Dobbins' Thuds were the first to officially introduce the wraparound camouflage finish (though the Vietnam era 'Ryan's Raiders' were the first to relinquish TO1-1-4 pale grey in favour of a darker underbelly, back in 1967). They also resurrected the aggressive 'Sabre Tooth' design (*Lindsay T Peacock*)

Below The Georgia Guard received a total of twenty-three F-105Gs and flew the type for some four years before converting to F-4Ds and subsequently to F-15 Eagles. Two Thuds were kept in storage for a year, according to the base historian MSgt 'Buddy' Gordon (a truck driver who's claim to fame is one of the world's biggest collections of Cola memorabilia). The unit's last sortie was flown on 25 May 1983, when Maj Duff Green flew F-105F 68-8299 (flight 'Peach 91') to Naval Air Station Patuxent River, Maryland (*Lindsay T Peacock*)

Above An evocative in-flight close-up of one of Georgia's Rebels. Dobbins played with Shrikes and 'iron' bombs, leaving the long-range 'heavy metal' in the custody of the active forces (*Lindsay T Peacock*)

Left Originally designed to accommodate nuclear bombs, the Thud's weapons bay was very quickly given over to additional fuel. An external rack or fuel tank could then be added, held in place with the assistance of some beefy steel straps which wrapped over the bay. This rare glimpse into the hydraulic line-crazed interior also shows the ALQ-105 blisters to good effect (*Peter E Davies*)

Defenders of the Crossroads

Below On 30 March 1981, the George-based 831st Air Division split its 130 Phantoms between the 35th TTW (responsible for F-4E training), and the newly reformed 37th TFW, nicknamed the 'Defenders of the Crossroads', which assumed control of the Weasel force. Its three squadrons comprised the 561st 'Blacks Knights', 563rd 'Aces', and the RTU, the 562nd TFTS 'Weasels'. Wing CO at the time was Col Luther E Thweatt (*Frank B Mormillo*)

Left A string of 'Aces' at George (*via Jim Rotramel*)

Right Bearing the diamond symbol made famous by the McConnell-based Thuds, a 563rd TFS F-4G shows off its matt, yet sun-glistened Vietnam-style tan and greens (*Frank B Mormillo*)

Above Up-and-away, tail 69-7287 tucks up its gear as it departs George. Built as McAir F-4-cum-number 3965 and still flying today, the machine was 'in the shop' at Ogden's hangar 3 between 20 May and 29 Sept 1978 to receive its Weasel-related alterations. Sadly, as of mid-1981 when this shot was taken, some five F-4Gs had already been 'struck' in accidents (*Jim Rotramel*)

Overleaf Wraparound camouflage finishes appeared during 1981 but were short-lived, despite the initial enthusiasm from the flyers. 69-0281 has 'popped' its receptacle ready for the boomer's probe (*Frank B Mormillo*)

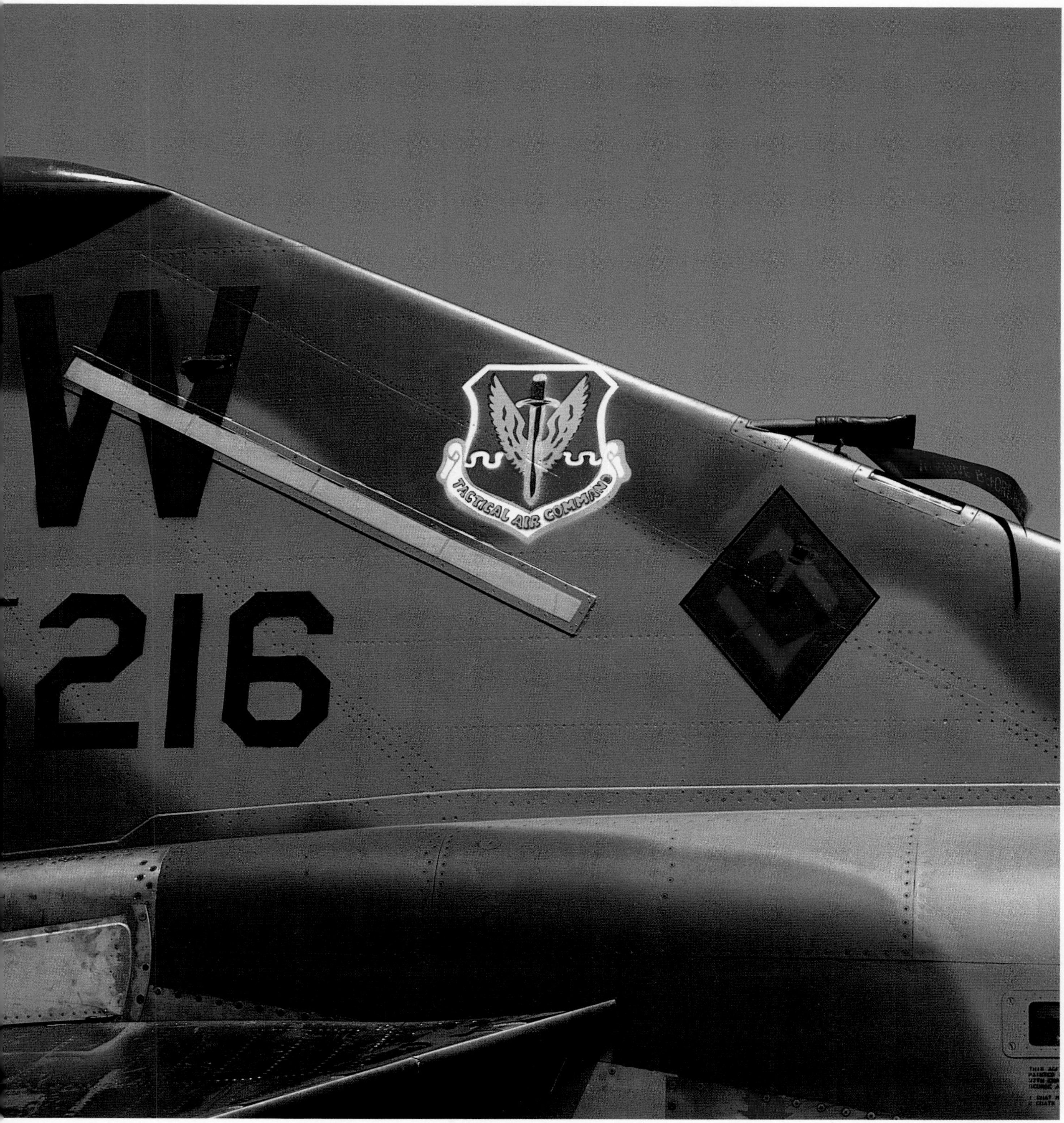
W
216
TACTICAL AIR COMMAND

Above Captured on celluloid during a December 1982 'Red Flag' outing, an F-4G contrasts beautifully with the snowy mountains below (*Frank B Mormillo*)

Right The Guard are in business as an F-4G lines-up to take on JP-4 from one of its KC-135 Stratotankers (*Frank B Mormillo*)

Above August 1983, and a 563rd TFS F-4G composes itself for landing at Nellis Tactical Fighter Weapons Center (*Frank B Mormillo*)

Right The 562nd TFTS has held down the role of 'Weasel' RTU for a decade. One of its most noted Bears was Ops Officer Lt Col Sam Peacock, an F-105 combat veteran highly skilled in the 'sixth sense' of flushing out sneaky radar sites. The 'Papa Bears' passed on their skills to the novice 'Baby Bears' over the Tonopah EW range in the Nellis Complex. A misjudged signal meant death in the real world (*Frank B Mormillo*)

Right A brace of well-armed lizard green-grey Weasels, a 'Golf' in the lead slot and an 'Echo' off his wing – bank over George on 8 May 1984. The European One camouflage was introduced during that year, replacing the tan-brown colour with slate grey (*USAF photo by MSgt D Sutherland*)

Above A 563rd TFS 'Ace' compresses its oleos, with the drag 'chute just about to pop out. The F-4Gs began to appear in the new Hill Gray 2 semigloss monochrome finish (named after Hill AFB, where the OOALC is located) during August 1987. At this juncture also the beasts were modernized under Phase One of the Performance Update Program (PUP), which introduced a new Unisys-developed Weasel Attack Signal Processor (WASP). This possessed eight times the memory of the old 64K HAWC, and was capable of processing threat data seven times as fast. The computer was subsequently redesignated the AN/APR-47. (Phase 2 of PUP, which was to add a new E-Systems Directional Receiver Group for added processing power and simultaneous narrow and wideband signal coverage, was abandoned owing to budget cuts). (*Frank B Mormillo*)

Peugeots & Pair-O-Dice

Below Phantoms do everything in twos. This brace from the 'Peugeots' are no exception as they depart Misawa AB, Japan, in October 1980 (*via Ben Knowles*)

Right Clean and mean and fresh from deep maintenance with a new coat of paint, a 'hunter-killer' F-4E heads for the ranges toting Mk 82 slicks, 'Winders and a GBU-10/B 'smart' bomb. Less obvious is the Pave Spike laser gun pod. F-4Es assigned to George's 'Cobras' (along with the 347th TFW at Moody and the 86th TFW at Ramstein) were also adept at 'squirting' lasers (*Mike Turner*)

Above The landing gear is often the focus of attention of F-4 crew chiefs. This fierce looking example shows off its digital Compass-Tie modified Westinghouse ALQ-119(V)17 noise/deceptor jammer to good advantage. The radar-zapper in the background is an AGM-45 Shrike (*Robert E Lee*)

Right The removal of the 20 mm 'Gat' as part of the 'sex change' enraged many pilots who had fought bitterly to get a six-shooter installed in the Phantom only a decade beforehand! 90th TFS aircrews pioneered the F-4E/G 'hunter-killer' concept, and once proven to be sound, Gat-gun Phantoms began to equip all Weasel squadrons, effectively doubling the size of the force! *Miss Piggy* was on the Clark Field roster (*Robert E Lee*)

Above ACM formed an important part of the multi-role Phantom crews' training programme, as evinced by this trolley load of Sidewinder AIM-9L/M air-to-air infrared-guided missiles (*Frank B Mormillo*)

Left The rear 'office' of F-4E 69-0305, with RHAWS and radarscope dominating the layout. This machine was originally operated by the RAAF on loan, did a stint with Nellis's F-4 Fighter Weapons School, was subsequently converted to F-4G status as the first of a follow-on batch of 18 Advanced Weasels, and redelivered to the 37th TFW on 12 June 1987 (*Jim Rotramel*)

Right A pair of slinky Weasels from the 'Pair-O-Dice', led by a silver F-5E Aggressor, trail-blaze over the lush Philippine backwoods. Their chief working area was the 44,000 acre Crow Valley range, some 15 miles north of Clark, the venue for 'Cope Thunder' and 'Cope Tora' manoeuvres (*via Robert E Lee*)

Above Clark's SEAD and dissimilar ACM squad in echelon, seemingly drifting over the Pacific (*via Robert E Lee*)

Overleaf Clark Field's 'Pair-O-Dice' accepted its first F-4Gs (69-0275 & -0279) at Ogden on 30 July 1979. Their departure from the Philippines twelve years later may have incurred the wrath of the gods!: Mount Pinatubo erupted on 12 June 1991 after having been dormant for 600 years, covering Clark Field in a thick layer of ash and pumice! The last of the F-4Gs had been phased out the previous month, with batches of six having departed the base from December onwards. Some of the returnees were held at George AFB; others have been reassigned to the 124th TFG, Idaho Air National Guard, at Boise, or shipped off to the 'boneyard' (*Frank B Mormillo*)

Spang's Warhawks

The Spang-based 'Panthers' transitioned from aged F-4C Weasels to the advanced 'Golf' model beginning on 28 March 1979, when 81st TFS CO Lt Col Duke Green and his EWO Capt Mike Freeman brought '239 in to a rapturous welcome. By 3 November the following year the 81st TFS had received its full complement of two dozen machines. Two of the beasts await clearance from the tower (*Kurt Thomsen*)

Afterburners ablaze, one of Spang's Advanced Wild Weasels roars down the runway. Crews now enjoy the luxury of the Polygone integrated range and its various sinister multiple threat emitter (MUTE) simulators – a far cry from the early days, when crews deployed to Lossiemouth in Scotland and 'worked' against the RAF's early-warning station at Spadeadam in Northumberland: 'one would hardly expect the enemy to keep his radars in one place and then put a big white radome on them!' Polygone was a massive step forward (*Kurt Thomsen*)

'Last Chance' means just that. Crew chiefs 'pull the pins' and give the aircraft a going-over just before takeoff. Gloved hands-on-canopy-frames ensures the safety of the groundcrew, who might otherwise get walloped by the inadvertent flip of a control surface or take the sharp end of a live weapon! (*Kurt Thomsen*)

Above left Heraldic symbols prevail in the USAF, and Phantoms of the 'Fighting Fifty-Second' wore this aggressive panoply of daggers on their starboard intake trunks (*Lindsay T Peacock*)

Above right The 'Panthers' intake insignia during the colourful era. The logo on the decal says Wild Weasel IV, but this smart design was employed on the F-4G also for several years (*Lindsay T Peacock*)

Right The 52nd TFW acquired F-4E 'six-shooters' (including DMAS ARN-101 digitally-enhanced versions) under Project Creek Realign, starting in September 1978, and flew the type alongside its F-4Gs until 1987, when the F-16C took up residence at Spang. In the early eighties the machines wore 'Vietnam wraparound' finishes, as exemplified by this aggressive example, nicknamed *Knight Stalker*, which was assigned to the 512th TFS 'Vigilante Pro Pace' at Ramstein. The 512th was dual-tasked with the Pave Spike/Maverick precision strike and nuclear Victor Alert missions, but frequently supported the Weasels (*Peter E Davies*)

Above Spang's F-4E/Gs were the first Weasels to sport 'low viz' sharkmouths, and formed part of the impressive line-up of Phantoms at Fairford in July 1985. The bird featuring the glossy grey nasal decor belonged to the 57th FIS 'Black Knights', a point interceptor outfit based in Iceland (*Tony Thornborough*)

Right Trailing cotton, a 480th TFS 'Warhawks' F-4G rolls out at Kleine-Brogel AB, Belgium, following a session at the 1986 NATO Tactical Air Meet. 'Warhawks' commander at the time was Lt Col Bil Hillman, a combat veteran who flew Phantoms out of Cam Rhan Bay, South Vietnam, during the turbulent war years in SE Asia (*Christian Gerard*)

Electric Weasels

The placard says it all. The base features all the mod-cons, including an array of TAB-Vee hardened aircraft shelters which tend to dwarf the rather tiny F-16 'Electric Jets' (*Christian Gerard*)

Above F-16C 86-255 stands alert in the 480th TFS dispersal. The first of the breed arrived at Spang on 23 April 1987 (*Christian Gerard*)

Right The 480th TFS 'Warhawks' still proudly bear their 'Red Squadron' logo even in this era where drab grey predominates the flightlines. The pristine nozzle of the General Electric F110-GE-129 derivative engine, capable of disgorging 29,000lb of thrust ($2\frac{1}{2}$ tons more than that generated by the Pratt & Whitney F100 used previously) is also evident (*Tony Thornborough*)

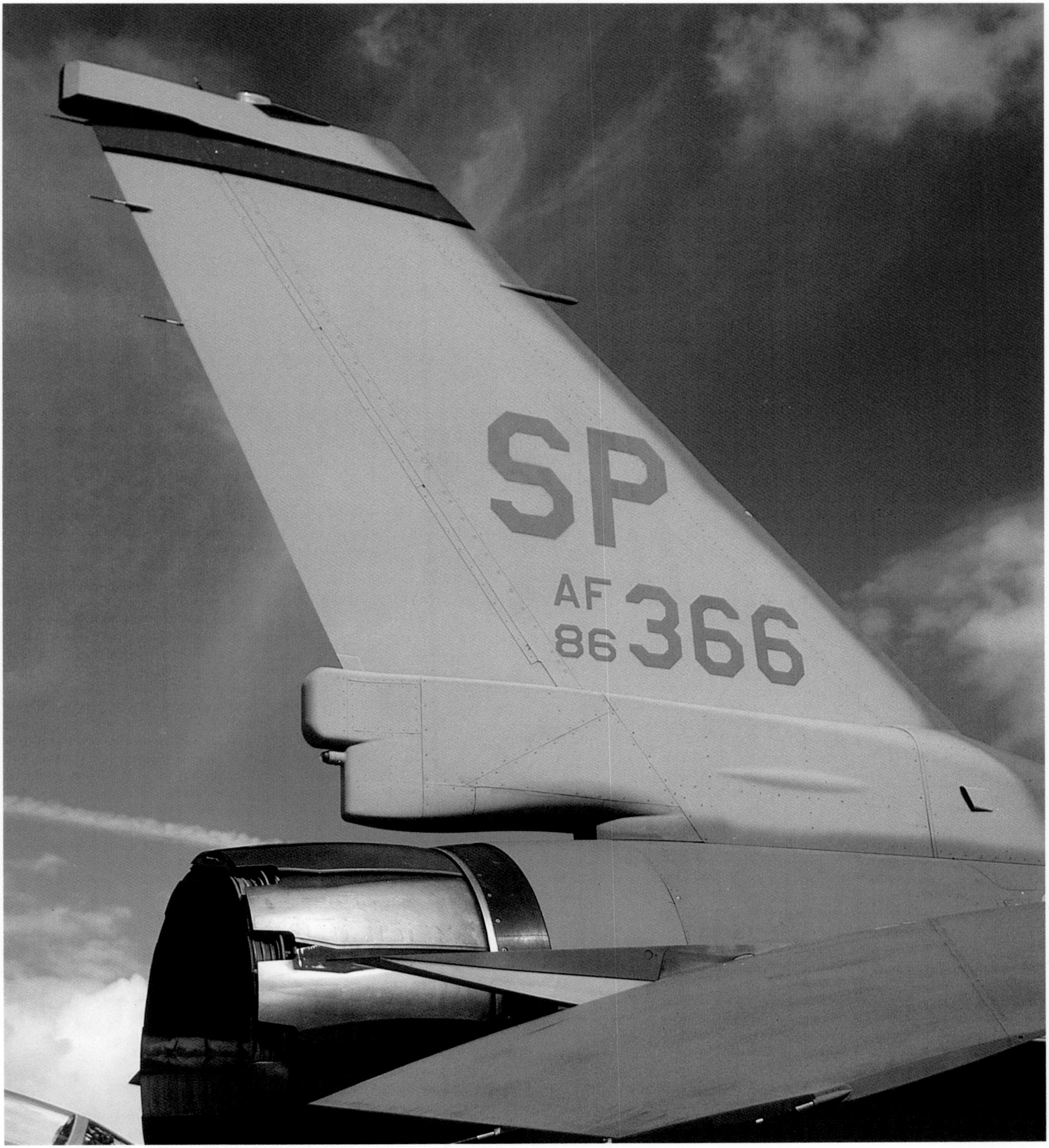
SP
AF
86 366

Above The current American penchant for avian titles lent the nimble F-16 the name Fighting Falcon, though many thought 'Shark' was more appropriate. The 'Electric Jets' assigned to Spang emphasize the point, and this example seems determined to gobble up one of the authors! (*Tony Thornborough*)

Right Big HARM, little bird. Spang's F-16Cs are not true 'Wild Weasels', but are certainly adept at the mission when working in concert with their PUP-updated Phantom brethren. The nimble 'Electra Jets' will soon sport the new Loral ALR-56M-Enhanced radar-receiving kit which provides the azimuth of enemy radars to within one degree – in theory, sufficiently accurate to usurp the venerable F-4G, but lacking the two-man crew which many deem so essential to 'Weaseling', not to mention the critical *range-finding* capability unique to the Phantom. The last 72 Block 50 F-16Cs to be built will be wired-up for the HARM-targeting system HTS pod, known colloquially as 'Weasel in a Can'! (*Tony Thornborough*)

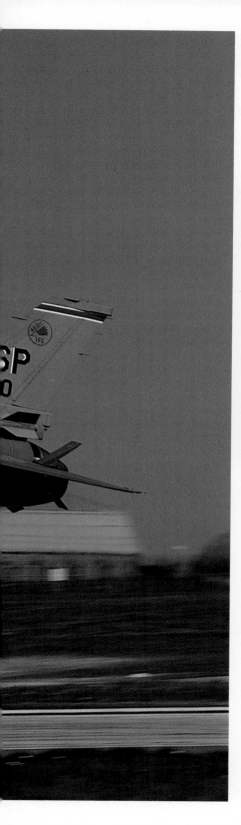

Above The new single-seat fraternity has its batch of twin-seat 'tubs' for 'Stan/Eval' sorties and other checkrides. Spang's three squadrons each possess a solitary F-16D, and '043 belongs to the 23rd TFS 'Hawks'. It was caught during its progress to the 11,000 ft active runway in October 1989 (*Christian Gerard*)

Left In a great show of wingmanship, a duo of 'Warhawks' prepare to burn rubber following a half-hour training stint, with airbrakes fully open (the Norwegians being the only F-16 operator to employ drag-chutes). The introduction of the 9G-capable 'Electric Jet' has created renewed emphasis in the ACM department, a role which tended to detract from the Weasel mission during the seventies, according to many an 'Old Crow' (*Christian Gerard*)

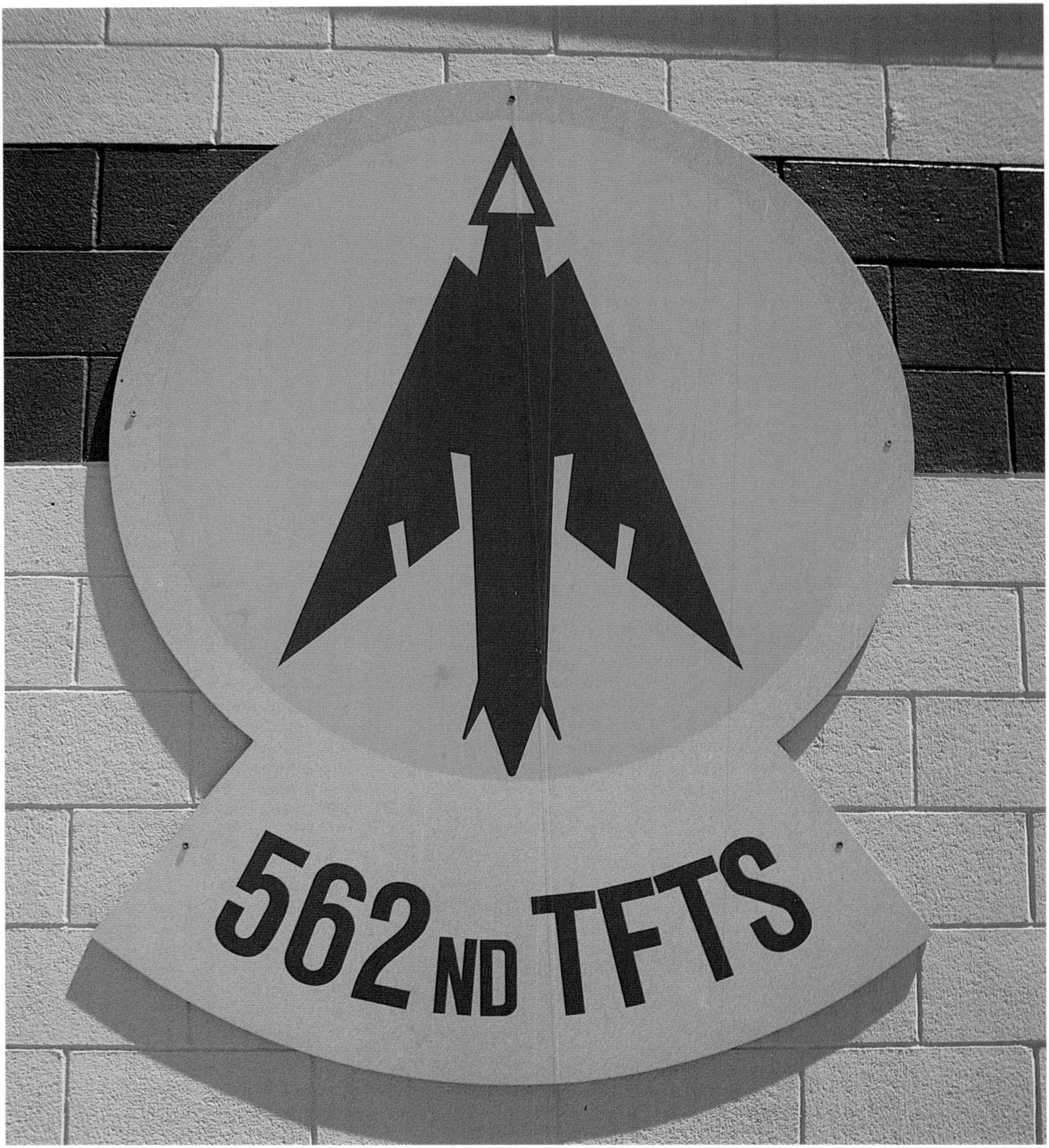
562ND TFTS

Willie Weasel College

Left On 5 October 1989 the Stealth Wing at Tonopah assumed the title 'Defenders of the Crossroads', and George's Phantoms were realigned under the 35th TFW, 831st Air Division, with Col Ron Karp in charge. The 562nd TFTS serves as the Replacement Training Unit for the USAF's dwindling Weasel forces (*Frank B Mormillo*)

Below All pods, knobs and slats and bearing the logos of George's Weasel RTU: the 562nd TFTS and its all-important Aircraft Maitenance Unit ... (*Frank B Mormillo*)

... and the same beast, in action, bearing a formidable load of HARM and Maverick missiles. Typical training sorties task the Weasels in flights of four to the secure Tonopah EW practice range within the restricted grounds of Nellis's huge inverted exercise triangle. Tonopah, named after the local 19thC silver-mining town, is perhaps better known as the home of the Lockheed Stealth fighters. The Weasels customary route is to head north by north-east for approximately 180 miles and then 'engage' the sites (*USAF*)

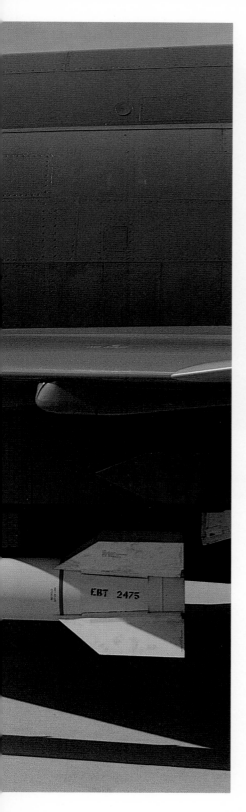

'Gaggle' insignia have become popular over the last three years. The 35th TFW comprises three training, one academic and one operational squadron. Those assigned with F-4Es include the 20th TFTS 'Silver Lobos' and 21st TFTS 'Cheetahs', while the newly concentrated, dedicated Weasel force comprise the 561st TFS 'Black Knights' and 562nd TFTS 'Weasels' (the 563rd TFS 'Aces' having already been disbanded at the time of writing) (*Frank B Mormillo*)

Above Black, golden-yellow, silver and blue adorn the pre-Gulf War flagship of the 35th TFW, F-4G 69-7574, reflecting its component squadrons
(*Frank B Mormillo*)

Right The sharp end of the F-4G. Removal of the 20 mm gun always proved controversial. When the original decision was made to do this, one high-ranking general (a MiG-killer in SEA) protested quite vociferously, but was told in no uncertain terms by a four-star to 'sit down and shut-up'! The alternatives — which included removing the radar and placing the antennae behind the radome, or fixing the system to the belly and wingtips — were rejected
(*Frank B Mormillo*)

Right The King-of-Phantoms at rest. Det 5's Weasels are customarily fitted with sunshades to ease radarscope and panoramic/homing indicator monitoring 'in the pit'. Maj Gen John A Corder, who heads the TAWC and who is considered to be the 'Wild Weasel Guru', will soon see his proteges disappear as the Weasel mission is given over to modified 'swing-role' F-16Cs, the operating costs for which will amount to about a third of that of the Phantoms. The one salvation is that all F-15Es are receiving a HARM-shooting capability alongside modified electronics, and these too will be 'embedded' in the new 'Super Wings' (*Frank B Mormillo*)

Above Detachment 5 of the Eglin-headquartered Tactical Air Warfare Center operates a trio of F-4Gs at George AFB. Originally pooled from 562nd TFTS machines, during July 1987 the unit snatched its own quota and daubed them with Oscar-Tango operational test unit identifiers. The 'F-4G Test Team' develops Weasel-related avionics, munitions and tactics as an adjunct to the Florida-based TAWC and Munition Systems Division. However, when the Weasel Fox-Four reached the end of its career, the annual RDT&E budget of $3–4 million was slashed (*Frank B Mormillo*)

Desert Stormers

A pilot checks-in at the 561st FS 'Black Knights' Operations Schedule desk prior to a sortie. The unit has a worldwide commitment and can be mobilized for action at 24 hours notice (*Frank B Mormillo*)

With the electric power and compressed air umbillicals from a A/M 32A–60A generator set connected, a Weasel crew accomplishes its 'Power On' checks. Once the engines are in motion this unit is disconnected, and the F-4G becomes a free agent. Crews may spend as much as an hour on the ground going through the checklists and built-in-test functions to ensure that all the systems are working 'as advertised' (*Frank B Mormillo*)

Above With a TTU hydraulic test cart dominating the camera frame, a Wild Weasel is prepped for a training sortie. Polishing the canopies is just one of the myriad preflight tasks undertaken by the seemingly indefatigable ground crew (*Frank B Mormillo*)

Right A Phantom 'stick' signals for 'chocks away', while his Bear buried in the 'pit' behind monitors his complex array of instruments. Originally, the F-4G's APR-38A HAWC could be selected to pick up threats at 5, 10 or 15 miles range, and then 'prioritize' them; this capability was substantially enhanced with the PUP Phase One mods (*Frank B Mormillo*)

Above A 561st AMU Crew Chief directs his 'baby' out its parking spot on the George AFB flightline. The 561st TFS deployed East to Shaika Isa in Bahrain on 16th August 1990 via Seymour-Johnson, North Carolina, as part of the early Desert Shield work-up. Their early presence in the theatre was deemed essential (*Frank B Mormillo*)

Right A taster of things to come: Red Flag 89-3 and a 561st TFS crew tries out its new Raytheon-mod AN/ALQ-184 ECM for size. The pod has been adapted from the old ALQ-119 and the latest versions feature a Rotman lens which increases Effective Radiated Power (ERP) by a factor of ten (*Jim Rotramel*)

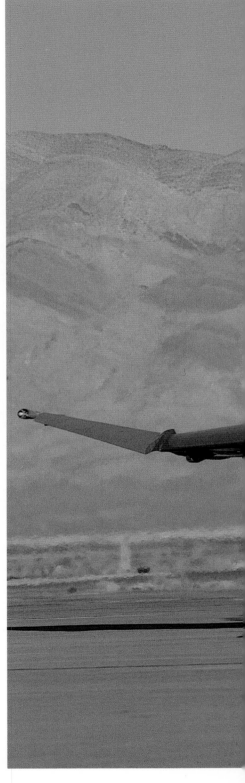

Left A svelte F-4E reveals its substantial armoury of AGM-45 Shrikes and AIM-7F Sparrows. Only the F-4Gs were dispatched to the War Zone, and among them was 69-7231, which generated 47 combat sorties/155 combat hours – the highest tally in the Wing (*USAF*)

Above The 'Black Knights' flagship rolls past the camera with a full complement of AGM-45 Shrike missiles. The APR-47-modified F-4G no longer uses the AGM-78 STARM, but the far more formidable AGM-88 HARM, along with the AGM-45 Shrike, AGM-65 electro-optically guided Maverick, and the usual gamut of cluster bombs (*Frank B Mormillo*)

Above Sgt Alan Martin was the assistant Crew Chief for F-4G 69-7263, nicknamed the *SAM slammer*. This machine, which was subsequently adorned in the commander's markings, was the first 35th TFW WIld Weasel to see action in the early hours of January 17th 1991 – the opening assault of the 44 day Desert Storm air war over Iraq and Kuwait. The beast was also George's highest scorer, having dispensed a lethal armoury of 37 HARMs, two Mavericks and one Shrike. Air and ground crews were scheduled for either day or night sorties, and Sgt Martin worked the night shift (*Frank B Mormillo*)

Right Equipped with 'wall-to-wall' AGM-88 HARM missiles, an F-4G heads for its prey. Aircraft were launched in this configuration for SEAD work over Kuwait; for longer-legged sorties over Iraq they carried a pair of missiles plus additional 370 US gal drop tanks. The one-piece windshield is a rarity (*USAF*)

Left The Phantom's jet nozzles became noticeably cleaner following Project Seek Smoke: the reworked turbojets comprise either J79-GE-17Es (low smoke only) or -17Fs (when incorporating Pacer Frugal reliability enhancements). The F-4Gs were the first in line to receive these improvements, along with the Eagle-type 600 US gal centreline tank, which extended G-tolerance to aircraft limits. Previously, F-4s had to jettison the centreline tank when 'mixing it up' with MiGs or SAMs. It was later retrofitted to the entire USAF 'Fox-Four' community under Technical Order 1F-4-1308 (*Frank B Mormillo*)

Above One of Spangdahlem's 'Panthers' tucks up its gear en route for the practice ranges. The parent 52nd TFW distributed its F-4Gs between its three squadrons during 1984, but reconsolidated them under the 81st TFS 'Panthers' upon their return from the Gulf (*Peter E Davies*)

Left A rare, uncensored glimpse at the 'pit' of the F-4G, combining the old with the new: old-fashioned needles-and-dials serve as the rearseat flight instruments, while the comparatively 'cosmic' cathode ray tubes, comprising the panoramic, homing and digitally-enhanced radar displays, with the banks of push-buttons, form the 'core' of the Weasel gear. The Bear is presented with the computer-prioritized threats and uses his right-hand multimode tracking handle to hand them off to a HARM missile, at the flick of a switch (*John J Harty*)

Above Home from the war, an F-4G from Spangdahlem's 'Gold Squadron' deploys its drag 'chute'—a tad sooty, but golden yellow, of course! (*Tony Thornborough*)

Lined-up at the home drome after having done some serious 'SAM-Slaying' in the Gulf. The 81st TFS deployed its Phantoms to Shaika Isa, Bahrain, on 5 September 1990 and received a dozen reinforcements drawn from the 480th TFS on 27th December. The 23rd TFS 'Hawks' deployed as a mixed F-16/F-4G unit to Incirlik AB in Turkey, to serve under Brig Gen Lee Downer's 4770th Combat Wing (the first 'superwing' to be created and tested in war). The aircraft returned to Spangdahlem on 5 April 1991, to be pooled in the 'Panthers' under the command of Lt Col Vinnie Cooper (*Christian Gerard*)

Left Spang's chief 'Radar-Zapper' was F-4G 69-7212, with 25 HARM launches to its credit. The 'torpedo' pod colours represent the 52nd TFW's three combat-ready squadrons: the 81st TFS 'Panthers', 480th TFS 'Warhawks' and 23rd TFS 'Hawks'. This beast came off McAir's production lines as an F-4E twenty-one years ago, and its aged but nevertheless still trustworthy airframe has seen service across the world: initially over the Australian Outback as one of two-dozen machines loaned to the RAAF (of which all 23 survivors were subsequently adapted to the Weasel configuration), and more recently in the Arabian Peninsula (*Tony Thornborough*)

Above Captain Jack Smart and his desert bush-hatted colleague (who is familiarly known by the not entirely inappropriate nickname 'Groucho'), pose near an 81st TFS steed at RAF Fairford, England (*Tony Thornborough*)

Above Lt Col Jim 'Uke' Uken was one of the EWO anchormen for the 81st TFS during its combat tour at Shaika Isa. In addition to being a Fighter Weapons School graduate with over 2000 hours in the 'Rhino', he was Chief of Tactics Development & Evaluation with Det 5 USAFTAWC, and mentioned that his father flew F-4s in SE Asia! Jim Uken's squadron flew 867 Desert Storm sorties (*Tony Thornborough*)

Left 'Groucho' gives the thumbs-up at the helm of F-4G 69-7212. The HARM missiles painted on the splitter plate – each of which epresents five weapons – serve as testimony to radar-killing exploits of the Weasels. Crews used beer brand call signs and yelled 'Magnum' whenever they launched an ARM; sometimes, by simply calling 'Magnum', every enemy active array would instantly shut-down shop, for fear of being shredded with the hundreds of steel tubes contained in the radar-homing missiles' warheads. At one point in the first three hours of Desert Storm, over 200 HARMs were airborne simultaneously! (*Tony Thornborough*)

Left and overleaf 'Weasels on the Wing', heading into the sunset. Sixty F-4Gs saw combat in the Gulf, for the loss of only one aircraft: on 19 January 1991, 69-7571 caught some light arms fire in its fuel tank. It subsequently ran out of gas while attempting an emergency landing in Saudi Arabia, and its crew punched-out. So successful were the Weasels, that earlier plans to retire the force have been shelved: the Air Force is extremely reluctant to see the huge 'institutional knowledge' possessed by the SEAD forces squandered in favour of short-term budget-balancing. Forty F-4Gs will be transferred to the Air National Guard – the 124th TFG at Boise, Idaho, and the 152nd TFG at Reno, Nevada – pending the introduction of the HTS-equipped F-16C and upgraded F-15E (*Dept of Defense*)